The History of Modern Egypt: From Napoleon to Now

By M. Clement Hall and Charles River Editors

ÁFGHÁN INTERIM GOVERNMENT
Public Health Ministry

The Health Ministry of the Afghan Interim Government wishes to show its appreciation to *MICHAEL HALL M.P.* for contribution of Medical Aid to the Afghan people in their time of greatest need.

J. Mojaddidi

Dr. Najibullah Mujaddidi
First Deputy Minister of
Public Health, AIG.

After service in the ranks of the British Special Air Service (SAS) Regiment, M. Clement Hall became a physician and then an orthopaedic surgeon. He has held professorial positions in Canada, Vietnam and the United States, practicing and teaching orthopaedic surgery in three continents and during several wars. Somewhere along the way, time was found to operate a four hundred acre mixed farm, a one hundred seat restaurant and to obtain a licence as a flying instructor.

Hall's time spent in the service and in the Middle East has provided extensive knowledge and a unique perspective of Egypt and the Middle East.

About Charles River Editors

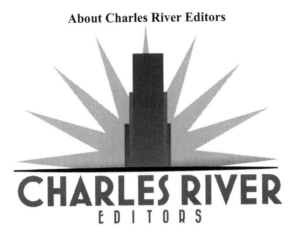

Charles River Editors was founded by Harvard and MIT alumni to provide superior editing and original writing services, with the expertise to create digital content for publishers across a vast range of subject matter. In addition to providing original digital content for third party publishers, Charles River Editors republishes civilization's greatest literary works, bringing them to a new generation via ebooks.

Visit charlesrivereditors.com for more information.

Introduction

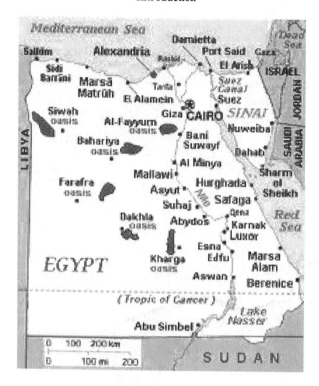

In the last year, Egypt has undergone a revolution that expelled its authoritarian leader of nearly 30 years and implemented elections that have pitted the Egyptian military in a power struggle with the Muslim Brotherhood, the long-time Islamic opposition group with ties to Hamas and elements of al-Qaeda. Making everything that much more surreal, the events have played out before well placed television cameras with continuous "real time" coverage of the revolution and ongoing turmoil, and foreign nations around the world eagerly await or dread the end result.

The situation in Egypt sounds messy today, but strife in Egypt is hardly a new occurrence. In fact, conflict has been more of a rule than exception since the end of the 18th century, when Western powers, beginning with Napoleon and the French, got involved in the territory that was at that point a part of the Ottoman Turkish Empire. Since then, European powers came into conflict with each other and local Egyptian officials in their imperialistic efforts, Egyptian nationalists tried to do away with foreign interference, and the critically important Suez Canal became a geopolitical hotspot. And when Egypt finally did receive full independence and sovereignty from the British, it was subjected to conflict between religious extremists, secular forces, pan-Arab nationalists, and oppressive strongmen.

The History of Modern Egypt comprehensively covers this turbulent history, helping to explain and sort through all the different forces at play in Egypt over the last 215 years. At the same time, it examines and analyzes all of the different religious, political, foreign, and military issues that continue to affect Egypt today. *The History of Modern Egypt* will bring readers up to speed on one of the world's crucial countries today.

The Origins of Modern Egypt

1798: Napoleon Bonaparte invades Egypt

Egypt was in disarray, and Napoleon thought a relatively easy victory over the English could be obtained by occupying Egypt and setting it up as a stopping point on the way to the ultimate goal of India. He proposed to the *Directoire* that such an invasion would not only embarrass England but would also support the interests of French trade. From a personal point of view, Napoleon could imagine himself following in the footsteps of Alexander the Great. The *Directoire* agreed to his plan, in part to rid themselves of Napoleon's presence, a threat to their own authority.

Bonaparte Before the Sphinx, by Jean-Léon Gérôme, 1868

A major armada was assembled in the Mediterranean ports under French control: 40,000 soldiers, 10,000 sailors, 13 ships of the line, 14 frigates and 400 transport ships. They sailed May 19th 1798, and on June 9th took Malta from the Knights of the Order of Saint John, who capitulated rather than fight an impossible battle.

Napoleon landed at Alexandria on July 1st, 1798, and defeated the Egyptian forces at the Battle of Subra Khit and then again, two weeks later, at the famous Battle of the Pyramids, where modern European infantry tactics – most notably the square formation – proved to be completely invulnerable to attacks by unsupported Egyptian cavalry. French losses were less than 30, while the Egyptians lost 2,000 men killed, further cementing Napoleon's status in the minds of his troops as an invincible general. The British Mediterranean fleet had been sighted, and after the soldiers had all disembarked, the French fleet withdrew from Alexandria to seek a better defensive position in Abukir Bay.

Napoleon's transport ships returned to France, while the battleships remained in Abukir Bay where Nelson and the British fleet found them 1st of August. Nelson split his ships, one section to each side of the French Fleet, between land and French ships as well as the open water. The battle lasted a few hours and the French fleet was totally destroyed, with only four of the 17 ships able to escape. Napoleon recognized he had lost his means of leaving Egypt and set about establishing himself in place as the ruler.

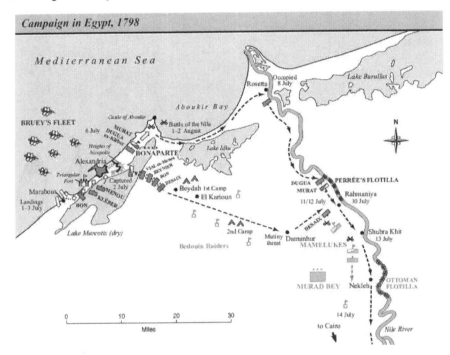

Napoleon made declarations of friendship, good intentions, and respect for religion; pilgrims travelling to Mecca were protected. A governing body, *diwan*, of local notables was set up, French civilising institutions were created: libraries, health services, museums and a zoo, dictionaries were made, newspapers founded.

His army, greatly diminished by disease as well as combat fatalities, was reinforced by 3000 sailors who no longer had ships, and they were needed to cope with the uprisings, starting with some slight ones before a major rebellion broke out on 22nd October 1798. This was suppressed with some difficulty and many French deaths; ultimately the rebels took refuge in the Great Mosque expecting a degree of mercy, but after shelling the mosque, the French soldiers broke in and killed all who were there. The *diwan* was abrogated, and replaced by French military rule. Many executions of suspected leaders followed the destruction of the mosque.

Napoleon also set about exploring the region for his own interests. He explored the Canal of the Pharaohs, the predecessor of the Suez Canal.

1799: Ottoman Response

Believing Napoleon was severely weakened by the British naval defeat, the Ottoman rulers mounted a campaign to displace him from their territory of Egypt. A two pronged attack was planned, by land from Syria and by sea from Rhodes, but Napoleon, when he heard the plan, pre-empted the land attack by marching his own troops into Palestine and capturing Arish in two days. He then moved on to the port of Jaffa, where in the early days of March his cannon destroyed the defences. The French soldiers were turned loose in the town, following the custom of the day when a town resisted rather than surrender. Following the precedent set by Richard Lion Heart at Acre, Napoleon murdered 4,000 prisoners rather than leave them behind to fight another day.

Plague began to visit his army at this time, with further loss of soldiers he could ill afford. He followed Richard's progress in reverse, going north up the Palestine coast, and like the early Crusaders found himself blocked by the defences of Acre. He had additional support from siege guns brought by sea, and since Ottoman reinforcements were on the way, he had to finalize the capture of Acre. Napoleon nearly achieved it, having entered the fortifications, but remarkably he was opposed by a fellow military academy graduate now fighting for the Ottomans, by crews from British ships, and the Ottoman garrison of Acre. In May he quit the assault.

The retreat from Acre is not as well known as the retreat from Moscow, but must have been as pitiful. At first the wounded and plague sick were carried, then they found this too much of a burden, so they killed their own men. All horses were given over for transport, and everyone walked, Napoleon among them. A scorched earth policy was executed, everything was destroyed in the wake of the army. By the time they reached Egypt, they had lost 1800 soldiers, two thirds to battle, one third to plague, and had as many wounded who managed to walk to Egypt. Those wounded who did not have the good fortune of dying were captured by the Ottomans, who tortured and beheaded them.

July 1799: Battle of Abukir and Napoleon's Departure

The Ottomans landed a substantial army and had reinforced their defensive positions at Abukir, but despite the pitiful state of his army, Napoleon went immediately on the offensive. It was estimated 10,000 Ottoman soldiers were drowned in their retreat, the remainder were otherwise neutralised; the leaders were captured and brought to Cairo as a triumphal Roman style procession of prisoners to laud Napoleon the victor.

In August, recognising the hopelessness of his position, Napoleon slipped away at night and with his three ships reached France without British interference. General Kléber reached an agreement with the Ottomans, the Convention of al-Arish, which was to allow the French soldiers to withdraw, but the British would not permit them to do so without surrendering. Kléber was assassinated, and his successor, General Menou, married an Egyptian woman, converted to Islam, and was comfortable in Egypt. He developed plans to improve industry and agriculture, plans that clearly would have to be supported by increasing taxes, and they came to nothing.

March 1801: An Anglo-Ottoman force occupied the Nile Delta. After a small amount of fighting the French concluded they had had enough, they capitulated to the British at the end of August 1801 and were repatriated to France in British ships.

From the campaign the British gained the Rosetta Stone and many antiques accumulated by Napoleon, while the French lost 30,000 soldiers. The Treaty of Paris in 1802 ended all hostilities between France and the Ottoman Empire.

Rosetta Stone and key

What did Egypt get from the French Invasion?

To Egypt in particular, and to the Muslim world in general, the superiority of western armies was painfully demonstrated. But from a cultural point of view, Egypt was brought into contact with French liberal thought and technology, and it also inherited the Napoleonic code of laws.

1801-1802: First British Occupation Of Egypt

The British had for the greater part been involved in sea battles around Egypt, notably the Bay of Abukir, but they did eventually land soldiers who in conjunction with Ottoman troops wiped up what remained of Napoleon's army before shipping the survivors home.

Under the 1802 Treaty of Amiens, British forces agreed to leave Egypt.

Restored Ottoman Suzerainty, 1801-1914

Mehmet Ali: The Founder of Modern Egypt

1805: Mehmet Ali (aka Muhammad; Mehmed; in Albania as Mehmet Ali Pasha; in Turkish as Kavalalı Mehmet Ali Paşa)

Mehmet Ali was of Albanian stock, born 1769 in Rumeli (which is today part of Greece). He came to Egypt in 1801, leader of a 300 man contingent of Albanian soldiers, as part of the force landed to oust the French invaders. To him is attributed the first of the internal actions to modernize Egypt, and from him was descended a long line of rulers.

During the first four years Mehmet and his Albanian soldiers remained in Egypt, there was an uncertain leadership in the region due to disputes between the *ulema* religious leaders, the remaining Mamluks, and Ottoman civil servants. Mehmet Ali entered into politics without showing his hand too clearly, but enough that in 1805 there was a clamor for the governor (*Wali*) to step down and be replaced by Mehmet, a decision to which the Sultan Selim III had to agree in March 1806.

The Mamluks were professional soldiers whose only interest was in being a warrior caste; originally of slave origin from the Caucasus, they had become a dominant force in the Ottoman Empire, and after the French left they conspired against all other civil authority. After Napoleon's departure and the British evacuation, they were still the feudal owners of Egypt, and their land was still the source of wealth and power.

Mamluk warrior

On March 1st 1811, Muhammad Ali invited all of the leading Mamluks to his palace to celebrate the declaration of war against the Wahhabis in Arabia, bringing between 600 and 700 Mamluks to parade in Cairo. Near the Al-Azab gates, in a narrow road, Ali's forces ambushed and killed almost all of them in what came to be known as the Massacre of the Citadel. During the following week, hundreds of Mamluks were killed throughout Egypt, and the death toll for Mamluks and their relatives throughout Egypt was estimated at 3,000.

Mehmet Ali's Reforms of Egypt

a) Nationalization of land: All Egypt was "nationalized." In this way the state owned all of the land, achieved by putting such high taxes on the tax collectors they had to capitulate and allow the land to be taken by the state. The government would decree what use the land would be put to, would allocate seeds, tools, fertilizer, control irrigation etc.

Cash crops were expanded from the traditional wheat to indigo, tobacco and cotton. The work was harder, but the pay was better, more labor was required and families increased in size commensurately, doubling the population.

French engineers were employed to create or improve the system of canals for irrigation, permitting three crops a year for each section of land.

b) All trade was conducted through the state; the state then sold on the commodities; as a result the farmers' income increased 400%, and "long staple" cotton thrived (an industry of importance to be discussed later).

c) Industry was aimed essentially at improving the capacity of the armed forces, but attention was given also to the needs for transportation – barge canals, river ports and roads were constructed. For agriculture, mechanisms were developed for weighing and storing grain, for refining sugar, for spinning cotton. The factories in Cairo made hand weapons, muskets and cannons. The shipyard in Alexandria began to build a navy.

The downside of this: factories need laborers; weapons need soldiers. Europeans were introduced as managers and teachers of industrial arts, peasants were drafted by a system of corvée labor to work in factories, to build the canals, to make the roads and to serve in the military.

Initially this was resented, machinery was sabotaged, but little by little an urban factory class developed, the work became better paid, and from them sprang the generation of professional classes, the doctors, lawyers, engineers and teachers.

d) Administration of government had been in the hands of the Mamluk class who had been eliminated; Mehmet Ali had to create a whole new class of bureaucrats. He divided Egypt into 10 provinces, and to a large part each was run by a member of his family.

e) The military had to be reformed, and this was accomplished in part by sending young officers to Europe, in particular France, for a military education, and then to rewrite military manuals in Arabic.

f) Education was promoted away from the usual schools which taught only the Koran to schools that taught the traditional broad range of subjects known in Europe, once again French was pre-eminent.

Military expeditions

Mehmet Ali was first and foremost a soldier, and his initial loyalties were to his employer, the Sultan of the Ottoman Empire, but only initially. The Saud family had moved from central Arabia to capture the holy cities of Medina and Mecca, and with that they began to enforce their Wahhabi doctrine. In 1803 Mehmet Ali conducted a campaign into Arabia and took the land from the control of the Saudis (who returned after World War I and took it back again). In the meanwhile, Hejaz came under Ottoman rule, reinforced by further campaigns conducted by his son Tusun, in 1811 and 1812. One campaign against the Saudis resulted in the capture and execution of Abdullah ibn Saud, the clan chief.

British Alexandria expedition of 1807

This was an attempt by the British to take Alexandria as a Mediterranean port to further the war against the French and the Ottoman Empire, with whom the French had now formed an alliance. 5,000 soldiers were landed, commanded by General Alexander Mackenzie-Fraser, and very little resistance was met until they advanced into Rosetta, where hidden snipers caused serious casualties and the British withdrew. In continuing action led by Mehmet Ali, some British were taken prisoner and were marched through a parade of their 900 dead comrades' heads mounted on sticks, but the live prisoners were not poorly treated.

Negotiations were held on a reasonably amicable basis, prisoners were released, and the British forces withdrew in ignominy.

Other Campaigns

Other campaigns led by Ali's numerous sons were conducted south of Egypt into the Sudan, Ethiopia and Uganda.

In 1821 the Greeks rebelled against the Ottoman rulers, and Mehmet Ali was asked to participate in suppressing the rebellion with Crete as the reward. Ali sent another son with 16,000 soldiers, 100 transports, and 63 escort vessels. Unfortunately for him, Greece had the European powers on their side, and on 20th October 1827 the entire Egyptian navy was sunk.

Despite that debacle, Mehmet Ali bounced back. A new navy was built, and a new army was recruited, trained and equipped. In October 1831 he was ready to pursue his dream of conquest of the Levant, which included part of modern day Israel, Lebanon and Syria. They would give him a skilled trading population, natural resources and trade routes; they would also bring him close to Anatolia, the mainland of the Ottoman Empire. An excuse for making war is generally de rigeur, and Mehmet Ali claimed Syria was sheltering Egyptians who were evading their civil or military obligations.

With that pretext, Ali won Syria easily in 1831, although Acre which only surrendered after a siege that lasted to May 1832. Ali then went on to enter Anatolia and defeat the Ottoman army at Konya in December 1832. The potential that he might take control of the entire Ottoman Empire greatly alarmed the Western powers who preferred the *status quo*, and in May 1833 the Convention of Kutahya required Mehmet Ali to withdraw from Anatolia and receive Crete (as the Sultan had first promised) and Hejaz (central Arabia) as compensation.

Mehmet Ali's end game

In 1831 Mehmet Ali advised the Western powers he would declare Egypt to be an independent country. The West was not pleased, and the Sultan resisted with military force, but his soldiers entered Syria and were soundly defeated at the Battle of Nezib in June 1839. Salt was rubbed into the wounds when their navy defected to join with Ali's.

When the Western powers ordered Ali to withdraw, he hesitated, and in response British and other European warships took up position on the Nile. In September 1840, they began shelling Beirut, and in November Ali reluctantly agreed to a severe reduction of his army and navy and to give up Crete and the Hejaz. As a compensation, he was granted hereditary rights as ruler in Egypt and the Sudan. Thus, Egypt became an autonomous province, but still within the Ottoman Empire.

By the time it was all said and done, the over-expenditure on military prowess left Egypt deeply in debt, to the tune of 2.5 million pounds sterling. Senility gradually overtook Ali, who ceased to rule in 1848 and died the following year.

Though Mehmet Ali is widely considered the founder of the modern Egyptian State, he never intended that Egypt would be ruled either by or for Egyptians. It was to be the "family business." As a result of his defeats of the Ottoman rulers, however, Europeans began to think of Egypt as an autonomous state.

After Mehmet Ali

1848, July-November: Ibrahim Pasha, acting governor

Ibrahim was Mehmet Ali's oldest son, and he assumed the power of *Wali* when his father was beyond the task by virtue of his mental deterioration. He had already demonstrated his capacity as a leader in military expeditions, but he ended up pre-deceasing his father.

IBRAHIM-PACHA

1848-1854: Abbas Hilmi I, governor

Son of Tusun, the next oldest male family member, and grandson of Mehmet Ali, Abbas became Regent of Egypt after his uncle Ibrahim died in November 1848, and then officially became the *Wali* when his mentally incompetent grandfather died in August 1849.

His reign was a mixture of undoing some of Mehmet Ali's progressive changes and supporting others. He discharged many of the long time advisers who had been used to doing things the French way. He undid trade monopoly agreements, reduced taxes, gave land away from state control, handed over factories to private enterprise, and reduced the size of the army (which was crippling the treasury).

One of his most important reversals of his grandfather's policies was to permit Egypt to become a transit point between the Mediterranean and the Indian Ocean by building a railway between Alexandria and Cairo in 1851. This shortened the four month trip around South Africa to India to six weeks. He also accepted an officer of the British Peninsular and Orient Shipping Line to produce in 1850 a detailed project for a canal.

Abbas' life ended July 1854 when he was murdered by his own palace guard.

1854-1863: Muhammad Said Pasha, Governor

The practice in inheritance of position was to appoint the oldest male member of the family, which explains why Abbas Hilmi, Muhammad Said's nephew, preceded him. Said, a son of Mehmet Ali, was appointed *Wali* after Abbas was murdered.

Unlike his brothers who had largely been concerned in military adventures, Said was educated in France, and among his friends was Ferdinand de Lesseps, who resigned his position in the French diplomatic corps and came to Egypt when Said unexpectedly came to power.

Ferdinand de Lesseps

Suez Canal

It had been well established long ago that there was no significant difference in the level of the Mediterranean Sea and the Red Sea, and that a canal between the two was feasible. Linant de Bellefonds, chief engineer of Egypt's Public Works, had made plans for a canal across the Suez isthmus, but Mehmet Ali wanted no part of it. Numerous other experts had tried to do the same, but Britain for some reason was opposed and preferred the Alexandria to Cairo railway which was built by Stephenson.

As his personal friend, though he was not an engineer, Ferdinand de Lesseps obtained from Said the right to form a company that would dig the canal, but international cooperation was required in the contract of the "Commission Internationale pour le percement de l'isthme des Suez." After extensive surveys, the Commission produced its report in December 1856. The British were opposed and the government dissuaded English investment, which impeded raising the anticipated cost of $40 million. Nevertheless the "Compagnie Universelle du Canal Maritime de Suez" was formed in December 1858 and work began April 1859.

It was de Lesseps friendship with Said that made the canal possible. When land was needed, Said saw it was made available. When labor was required to dig the canal by hand, 20,000 workmen a year, Said saw that forced (corvée) labor was made available without being too concerned about anti-slavery laws in force. When de Lesseps was out of funds, his friend Said chipped in with the purchase of more of the company's shares. When the Ottoman government interfered with the use of slave labor, Said produced Egyptian government funds for industrial excavation equipment. De Lesseps was belatedly required to "treat the natives well – they are men", and with that worker conditions improved. The British, ever willing to criticise the French, made official complaints about slave labor, to which de Lesseps responded by pointing out the British had been a lot less particular when they were building their railway.

The Suez Canal would open after 10 years of construction in 1869.

Reforms

Said followed a program of encouraging European investment and participation in Egyptian life, and many from the professional classes settled in Alexandria and Cairo, with the resulting European style housing present today. An objectionable side effect were the "capitulations", which exempted foreigners from the rule of Egyptian law and obligations to pay taxes, and encouraged a less than desirable expat community development.

Egyptians were given the opportunity to buy land and a middle class developed. The Sudan benefited by the official banning of slave raiding, but unofficially this still occurred.

In 1854 Said established the Bank of Egypt as the country was going into debt, partly as a result of the support of the Suez Canal; by 1863 the foreign debt was $30 million.

Cotton

The American Southern States of the Confederacy depended on "King Cotton" for their economic well-being. An idea was devised that if they failed to ship cotton to England, a large part of whose workforce were dependent on the manufacture of cotton goods, then England would be forced to join in the Civil War on the side of the Confederate States. So they introduced an embargo on themselves; cotton was stored in the warehouses and bonds were sold, much as a commodity market is operated today. However, as the South hoped to harm England's economy in particular, the British had managed to stockpile plenty of reserve cotton, and ultimately the effect of the South's ban was to create a greater demand for cotton grown elsewhere. During the American Civil War, the demand for Egyptian cotton boomed, introducing a false sense of hope into the economy. Egypt incurred debt, but when the American Civil War ended, the demand for Egyptian cotton fell off even as the foreign debt remained.

1863-1879: Khedive Ismail

Son of Ibrahim, grandson of Mehmet Ali, educated in Europe, fluent in French; all of this made Ismail seem a good candidate for the job. When he inherited the post of *Wali,* Egypt was doing very nicely with its trade in raw cotton, thanks to the American Civil War, and that was his downfall. It's hard not to draw a parallel with the easy money that led to a 21st century building boom in parts of Europe, and the easy seduction of bankers offering money.

After he returned to Egypt he was given a number of responsible diplomatic tasks, including a mission to the Pope, to the Emperor of France (Napoleon III), and to the Ottoman Sultan. He was given the military responsibility in 1861 of leading an expedition into the Sudan to suppress an uprising.

Khedive of Egypt

Khedive is a term of Persian origin and approximately equal to "prince." It is a title of more significance than *Wali*, and it was at first refused by the Sultan but later granted in 1867. Ismail also obtained from the Sultan decrees (*firman*) that inheritance of title would be from father to son (no longer the oldest male), and a grant of virtual independence of Egypt from the Ottoman rule. Needless to say, these came at a price. Egypt would also have the right to float loans without first obtaining Ottoman permission, and that created its own price.

Reforms

Some of the changes he made:

Bureaucracy: remodelled the customs system and the post office; established an assembly of delegates in November 1866, though anticipated as an advisory body and not executive.

Education: school systems were improved.

Communications: telegraph lines were erected.

Culture: Egyptian Museum, National Library, Geographical Society, opera (commissioned Aida) and a theater, landscape gardens in major cities.

Industry: stimulated commercial progress, created a sugar refining industry, improved cotton trade.

Edifices: built palaces, greatly expanded Cairo, building a new quarter modelled on Paris, and Alexandria was also improved.

Transportation: He launched a vast railroad building project in Egypt and Sudan; canals were dug, bridges were built.

Social changes: reduced slave trading and extended Egypt's rule in Africa.

Geographic changes: In 1874 he annexed Darfur, but was prevented from expanding into Ethiopia after his army was repeatedly defeated.

War with Ethiopia

Ismail had delusions of empire building to encompass the entire region of the Nile, down into its source in Abyssinia (Ethiopia) and the western borders of the Red Sea. He believed also that Abyssinia was fertile land that would feed the increasing population of Egypt.

He did succeed initially in establishing territorial gains, accepting grants of territorial control from the Ottoman Empire in 1865, and by 1872 he had established huge cotton plantations in territory stretching to the Red Sea. But all his dreams came to an end with military defeat in 1876 by the Abyssinian army. In 1884 with the Anglo-Egyptian-Ethiopian Hewett Treaty, the land he had taken was surrendered (only to be seized by Italians in 1890 and designated Eritrea).

Suez Canal

The canal started by his predecessor, was officially opened by Said to great acclaim and presence of royalty in November 1869. It had (of course!) cost twice the original estimate. The first commercial ship to use the canal was the British P&O *Delta*, and although the British government had done all they could to obstruct the canal, the P&O suggested it long before it became a fact.

Still, the canal was not an immediate financial success, and deeply in debt Isma'il Pasha was obliged in 1875 to sell his shares for £4,000,000 to the United Kingdom.

Debts

Just as in the 21st century, the Faustian bankers and the major European powers had loaned money to Egypt at the height of the cotton boom, now falling away after the Civil War concluded, and they wanted their money back. Ismail had expended it on the Suez Canal, on his buildings and railways, and on his war with Ethiopia. The national debt had climbed from 3 million to 100 million pounds sterling – and there was no money. He sold his shares in the Suez Canal for 4 million pounds, and that barely touched the debt.

A Public Debt Commission was established in 1876, and the Khedive agreed to a Commission composed of representatives of the governments of Britain, France, Italy and Austria to investigate his financial obligations. Following further loss of finances related to low water levels on the Nile and the Russo-Turkish war, the Khedive submitted his finances to joint French-British "Dual Financial Control": they would collect the taxes and control government expenditure. The Khedive humiliated himself by adding English and French Ministers to his cabinet, and appointing an Armenian as Premier. In 1878 he turned over his personal estates to the nation, and accepted he was now a mere constitutional sovereign.

It was at this point he made his declaration, "My country is no longer in Africa; we are now part of Europe. It is therefore natural for us to abandon our former ways and to adopt a new system adapted to our social conditions." It may well have had a bitter twist to it. Although the larger cities had developed distinct European flavors, most Egyptians lived in poverty, were illiterate, and suffered hard labor and heavy taxation.

Nationalist Resistance

The debt commissioners did at the end of the 19th century what the Spanish and Greek governments are doing at the start of the 21st century. They cut expenditure on public works, education and the military, they delayed payments on everything, and of 2,600 officers, 1,600 were to be retired. Street demonstrations quickly followed.

Khedive Ismail resumed control and ordered the soldiers back to barracks, sent the European ministers home, and appointed a new cabinet with his son, Prince Tawfiq at its head, and a competent though westernized minister, Sharif, to draw up a new constitution. Pay cuts were rescinded, but the debt remained.

France proposed a military occupation of Egypt, which Britain opposed, not because "it wasn't nice" but because they wanted no other power between England and India, and France had just been beaten by Prussia. Germany demanded the Ottoman Sultan should depose Ismail and replace him with Tawfiq.

Ismail received telegrams from the Sultan in Istanbul, addressing him as "ex-Khedive," and informing him there was no further need for his services. Two days later he was on his way to Naples.

1879-1892: Khedive Tawfiq

Tawfiq was Khedive Isamail's oldest son, and he led an unremarkable life without any public office until he was appointed in 1878 to be head of the cabinet council when Ismail was forced into the position of constitutional sovereign. He was quite unprepared for office when his father was deposed.

The new khedive was so displeased by the news of his accession that he struck the servant who first brought the tidings to him. Egypt and Sudan at that time were involved in financial and political troubles brought about by the policy of Ismail, and the situation was made worse by the inaction of Britain and France for some months following Tewfik's accession. He found general disaffection throughout the now impoverished country, and he knew and saw no way to alter that.

In November 1879, the "Dual Control" was re-established, but the Egyptian cabinet no longer had any foreign ministers. In 1880 the Commission was taking 50% of the nation's taxes to repay debts to foreign interests, with consequent slashing of budgets for all public services. The foreign expats, which included Turks and Circassians, who were living in Cairo and Alexandria, continued to be exempt from taxation

Urabi revolution

January 1881, Colonel Ahmad Urabi led a delegation of officers to Prime Minister Riyad. The War Minister planned to arrest them, but this was pre-empted by their soldiers storming the building to rescue their officers. Better conditions were promised for the military and the War

Minister was replaced.

In September there was a further threat against Urabi, but in a face-off with the Khedive Tawfiq backed down, the cabinet was dismissed, a new constitution was to be written, and all the retired officers were called back to duty with the army.

Colonel Urabi

For the first time, the new constitution gave executive power to the legislative assembly. Urabi was a national hero, but the expat community was concerned about the rise in military power, and European governments began to threaten occupation. The Egyptians were not dismayed and became assertive, and in response Britain and France sent warships.

However, the Ottomans had lost large areas of their territory in the war with Russia and were not open to losing more to European countries. In June 1882 there were riots in Alexandria, which were suppressed by the army at a cost of 3,000 Egyptian lives, including 50 expats killed or wounded. The British ordered the Egyptians to dismantle the defensive works at Alexandria, seized their tardiness as an excuse and shelled the city, while the French ships withdrew. Alexandria was on fire, and the English landed to extinguish it.

Tel-el-Kebir and aftermath

The Egyptian cabinet meeting in Cairo declared war on Britain, but the British fleet entered the Suez Canal, landed soldiers at Ismailia and on September 10th 1882 fought an indecisive engagement at Kassassin. On September 13, the British under General Wolsey confronted the Egyptian army under Colonel Urabi at Tel-el-Kebir. Knowing the Egyptians would be asleep at night, General Wolsey ordered an unusual frontal assault at night, beginning at 5:45 a.m. before daybreak. The Egyptians were taken by surprise, the battle was finished by 7:00 a.m., and the losses were 57 British and 2,000 Egyptians. The British cavalry now rode towards an undefended city of Cairo.

Urabi surrendered, Wolseley arrived in Cairo by train, Khedive Tawfiq was reinstated, Urabi was exiled to Ceylon, and the British were firmly in charge. From that time forward the British took control of the Egyptian army, trained according to British standards and commanded by British officers.

Sudan

While the British were wondering what to do with their army in Egypt, the *mahdi* ("rightly guided one", a soubriquet adopted by Muhammad Ahmad) revolted against Egypt, and a British force sent to relieve Khartoum was ambushed. Still, the British decided it was not yet the time to withdraw their army.

In November 1882, the British abolished the Dual Control, and Lord Dufferin was sent out to report on the dire financial straits of Egypt, on which claims were now being made for destruction of property in Alexandria, and the costs of support of the British occupation. The army was virtually shut down, public expenditure was slashed and schools were closed.

Making matters worse, in 1883 a cholera epidemic broke out, and here the Khedive came into his own, going with his wife to Alexandria to visit and encourage the sick in the hospitals.

In 1884, Sir Evelyn Baring (later Lord Cromer) was sent to Egypt as diplomatic agent and Consul-General of Britain; he had previously served as one of the debt commissioners and was more than familiar with the problem; he was to remain in Egypt for the next 24 years. Baring sought to improve Egypt fiscally by improving the lot of the peasantry, the bulk of the population. This he thought could be achieved by reduction in taxation on sheep, goats, grain weighing and salt, reduction of forced labor, and improvement in irrigation. British engineers worked to improve existing systems since there was no money for new ones, and with their assistance there followed improved irrigation and a dramatic rise in agricultural production. In five years the tide against national bankruptcy was turned.

Baring encouraged Tewfik to show his activity in administration of his country, and he showed a genuine desire to govern Egypt for its own benefit. He accepted the importance to Egypt of British assistance and support, and he held himself aloof from any palace intrigue.

Meanwhile, the war in the Sudan was not going well, Gordon and thousands of Egyptian troops were killed by the rebels, known to Kipling and the British Tommies as "fuzzy-wuzzys", and the British pulled out of the Sudan. They were contemplating pulling their army out of Egypt altogether, on the proviso they would re-enter if a revolution required it; however, since French conspirators whispered that meant they would come back when and how they wished, the end result was they didn't leave at all.

1892-1914: Abbas Hilmi II, khedive

Suddenly and unexpectedly, Tewfiq died in his Helwan Palace, close to Cairo, on 7th January 1892. His oldest son, Abbas, succeeded him.

Abbas as a youth had been taught by British tutors in Egypt, but he was a 17 year old student at an Austrian military academy when he unexpectedly inherited the position of Khedive. By manipulation of calendar differences between the Muslim lunar months and the Christian Gregorian system, it was calculated he had reached his 18th birthday, and was therefore not in need of a Regent. With that, there was no official reason for Ottoman interference in British interests in Egypt.

From the outset, Abbas had difficulty grasping that he was not free to do as he wished, that Egypt was under British control, and that he was obliged to work with them. It was suggested that the difference in age between Abbas and Baring had something to do with this, and Abbas may have resented the "fatherly" attitude, equally it is probable as a young man newly come to power he did not realize its limits. In January 1893, Abbas appointed a nationalist as prime minister, forcing the pro-British prime minister (Mustafa Fahmi) out of office. Baring called for more troops to be sent from Britain, and to resolve matters Abbas and Baring compromised with a third candidate, veteran politician Riyad.

There was another *faux pas* when Abbas criticized British led units of his own army. When Kitchener offered his resignation, Baring (now Lord Cromer) through Prime Minister Riyad required a public apology from Abbas, which was resentfully given. Abbas was learning his place the hard way.

Britain's military position in Egypt

The British military presence had been reduced from 20,000 to 5,000, but there was no legal basis to justify their presence, no matter how slight the number. There was no agreement with the Ottomans, nor Egypt, nor international treaty to justify their continued occupation of Egypt. The khedive, however, understood they were his support against rebellions, and the population at large was indifferent. Still, some nationalist movements were afoot in the late 19th century, usually comprised of the educated classes who had been taught by Europeans, and who "worked with words" as lawyers, journalists and teachers themselves. They wanted the foreign occupying troops to leave their country.

Society for Revival of the Nation

Mustafa Kemil

Mustafa Kemil as a student had led anti-British protest marches. He chose the French law school in Cairo, in part because Egypt had inherited the Napoleonic code of laws since the time of the French invasion, and the British had never seen reason to change them. He went to France to continue his studies in Toulouse, and was host to a banquet celebrating the Sultan's accession day, secretly funded by the khedive.

Unsurprisingly, his anti-British sentiment found support in France, but also from Constantinople. Back in Egypt, he founded the secret "Society for the Revival of the Nation" with the khedive as a leading member, which later became the National Party. He was not inclined to armed rebellion, he played with pan-Islamism which European countries universally feared, and as Abbas aged, matured, and came to accept the English assistance to his country, Kemil and Abbas went their separate ways. He died from tuberculosis at the age of 33, his funeral procession drew mass crowds, and he had left his mark.

As Egypt's debt diminished, as the country became more prosperous, European investment returned and a larger class of expats developed. As in British India, when the wives came a gulf was established between the "natives" and the Europeans, with their own clubs and societies into which the Egyptians had no right of entry. Resentment mounted. The British, although they assisted in the development of agriculture, were not interested in assisting industry which might compete with factories in Britain, so Egypt was to produce raw goods such as cotton but not be permitted to weave it. Schooling was kept at a low level, and English was to replace Arabic as more suitable for understanding science.

Taba Affair

The British regarded Sinai as part of Egypt, a useful buffer between Ottoman held Syria and the Suez Canal. Abbas gave control of the eastern shore of the Gulf of Aquaba to the Ottomans while retaining the western shore, but the Ottomans encroached on this by building a fort at Taba to the west side. British gunboats in the Gulf persuaded them otherwise.

Gulf of Aqaba

The surprising reaction of Egyptian nationalists was against their own country's interests and in favor of the Ottomans, because they thought the British were only looking after British interests and Istanbul was their real protector.

Denshawai Incident

Another affair in June 1906 typified the arrogance of the British officer and the helpless attitude of the Egyptians who had no choice but to tolerate them. Some officers on a shooting party entered a village with the intention of shooting pigeons, and in response the villagers explained they liked their pigeons and the pigeon manure in the barns was valuable. The British shot at them anyway, starting a barnfire. As the villagers tried to disarm the officers, a gun was discharged probably by accident and a village woman was wounded and four others struck with birdshot. The officers panicked, two ran away, and one was overcome with heat stroke and died. The rescuing soldiers thought the peasant who was supporting the dying officer was responsible and beat him to death.

The colonial powers would not leave well enough alone. The next day, 52 villagers were arrested, a summary trial convicted them of murdering the officer who had died of heat stroke, and four were sentenced to death by public hanging. Others were sentenced to penal servitude for life, terms of hard labour and public flogging. All of this despite the evidence of the Egyptian police official who accompanied the soldiers to the village and testified that after the woman had been shot, the officers fired twice more into the mob. He was sentenced to two years imprisonment and 50 lashes for his intransigence.

There was widespread disapproval, as much by liberal Englishmen as by nationalist Egyptians, which did much to strengthen the hand of the Nationalist Party. After the death of Mustafa Kemil, the party split between a number of leaders with diverging views. To control them, the government in 1909 required newspapers to be licenced, but ways around this, some taking advantage of Capitation laws, were found by those protesting British rule.

Sir Eldon Gorst and Lord Kitchener

As he aged, Abbas became more accepting of the British presence, and in their turn the British began to loosen the reins. In 1900 Abbas paid a second visit to Britain, during which he said he thought the British had done good work in Egypt and declared himself ready to cooperate with the British officials administering Egypt and Sudan. His relations with Cromer's successor, Sir Eldon Gorst, were excellent, and they co-operated in appointing the cabinets and in checking the power of the Nationalist Party.

However, when the Prime Minister was murdered by a young member of a secret society bent on mass extermination of those who collaborated with the British, there was further inhibition of transfer of powers to the Egyptians. Moreover, Gorst, struck with cancer, resigned in 1811.

The appointment of Kitchener to succeed Gorst displeased Abbas, and relations between him and the British deteriorated. Kitchener often complained about "that wicked little Khedive" and wanted to depose him. He took a strong stand against nationalists but was genuinely interested in improving the lot of the peasantry and in representative government.

When the Ottoman Empire joined the Central Powers in World War I, the United Kingdom declared protectorate status over Egypt on 18th December 1914, deposed Abbas, and replaced him with his uncle, Hussein Kamil. Hussein died in 1917 and was followed by Fuad.

By then, the British took over Egypt completely, using it as the base from which to launch military attacks into Ottoman occupied Syria. The country was swamped with British and Dominion soldiery who behaved like soldiers always do. The agriculture was changed to growing wheat, animals were commandeered, and young men were conscripted to be auxiliary troops. All of this contributed to growth in nationalist, anti-British, feeling.

Ambiguous Independence, 1918-1945

Britain took Egypt for granted, and after the war, when moves were afoot to break up the Ottoman empire, no thought was given to Egypt. Representatives of Arabs, Jews and Armenians were invited to the peace conference, but Egypt was not.

The Egyptians thought to send a *wafd* (delegation) and the name of Saad Zaghlul was prominent. He had a history of arrest for belonging to a nationalist movement, then went to France to study law, and after returning to Egypt to practice law was made a judge. His career was also helped by friendship with a princess, his marriage to the Prime Minister's daughter, and the friendship of Lord Cromer.

Saad Zaghlul

Saad became Minister for Justice in 1910 but quit over differences two years later; when Kitchener made arrangements for a Legislative Assembly in 1913 he was successful as a candidate and in January 1914 was appointed Vice President of the Assembly. However, the

Assembly was suspended at the outbreak of war, never to meet again.

The Assembly was replaced by an unofficial Wafd party, on whose behalf at the end of the war Zaghlul met with the British High Commissioner, Sir Reginald Wingate (older cousin of Orde whom he influenced), to enquire in regard to Egyptian independence. They were brushed off by the Foreign Office, and after Prime Minister Rushdi resigned no one would take the office. The Wafd received 100,000 signatures in support, unrest mounted, and with that the British exiled Zaghlul to Malta.

In response to Zaghlul's exile, a major uprising took force. Students went on strike, shops were looted, railroad tracks blown up, telegraph wires cut; and rioters were killed or injured. To show the ecumenical nature of the protests, Coptic priests appeared in the mosques and Muslim preachers stood in the pulpits. The army and the police quelled the riots, but General Allenby, the new High Commissioner, sensibly ordered the return of Zaghlul from Malta.

The British appointed Lord Milner to negotiate in 1920 in London with Saad Zaghlul, and a prospective document of quasi-independence was offered. However, Saad Zaghlul would not accept it, and the British government rejected it.

Britain's Declaration of Independence for Egypt

Allenby persuaded the British government to advise Sultan Fuad they would negotiate with a delegation of his picking, and Fuad selected Adli Yakan. However, when the negotiations collapsed, Saad (who now represented the "spirit of national dignity") was exiled once more, leading to further strikes and riots.

Once again, Allenby's good sense and sympathetic judgement prevailed. After discussions in London, he returned at the end of February 1922 with a formal statement ending Britain's protectorate and declaring Egypt to be a quasi-sovereign state: there were clauses regarding provisions for communications and war, and there were 200,000 foreigners in Egypt who ran most everything that mattered, including the army. The foreigners continued to be protected from Egyptian law by the Capitulation treaty, meaning Egypt did not have total sovereignty.

Constitution

In 1923 the Egyptian lawyers produced a Constitution modelled on that of Belgium. Fuad was now King Fuad, but with limited powers. In April 1923 the British terminated martial law, Saad returned to Egypt, and so did other long-exiled nationalists. The Wafd became a political party with an overwhelming majority in the Chamber of Deputies, and Saad was Prime Minister, but for all the outward appearance of normalizing relationships, secret ultra-nationalist parties remained.

In November 1924 Sir Lee Stack, commander of Egypt's army and governor of the Sudan, was murdered by terrorists. Enraged, Allenby demanded retribution from Saad, prosecution of the assassins, a sum equivalent to $2.5 million, and withdrawal of Egyptian troops from the Sudan. Saad resigned, and King Fuad appointed a new cabinet.

Early years of Independence

In the post-war state of quasi-independence there were three major forces in Egypt. King Fuad, a constitutional monarch, wanted more power than the constitution awarded him, the Wafd party dominated the Chamber of Deputies, and the British still ran almost everything. There were lesser Egyptian political parties and there were large landholders who, although not organized as a party, held substantial powers. As the population grew, there were more landless peasants, but more major landholding landlords (the royal family owned 10% of the land), an overdependence on cotton damaged the economy, and even that was jeopardized by the new artificial fibers, and the dreaded boll-weevil. And education had become its own enemy, a class of young persons had been educated away from the peasantry but there were no "clean hands" jobs for them, and the Depression was on its way.

Anglo-Egyptian Treaty

Egypt found itself uncomfortably situated between Libya and Ethiopia, both occupied by Fascist Italy; although King Fuad supported the Italians, the Wafd did not. But Fuad died in 1936 and was succeeded by his 16 year old son Farouk, and an agreement was reached whereby Britain would continue a 20 year occupation of the Canal Zone, restrict the military to 10,000, and the despised Capitulations would be abolished.

World War II

When the war started there were 60,000 Italians in Egypt, and the Egyptians realized if the British left, the Italians would come. The Italians were altogether too conveniently arranged between Libya and Abyssinia with the highly desirable Nile valley.

The Italians were defeated in North Africa by General Wavell, but then the Germans came in force to support them under the Desert Fox, Rommel, who drove the British back to El Alamein on the Egyptian border. At this point some Egyptians thought they would make an arrangement with the Germans ,and the British distrusted Farouk, so they surrounded his palace with armoured cars and advised him either to abdicate or to form a pro-British government. This repeat of subjection to the British caused unrealistic resentment at the time. After all, if it wasn't going to be the British, it would be the Italians and the Germans.

Surprisingly Egypt prospered during the war, a byproduct of the fact the military needed goods and services. With that there was increased employment, and the entertainment industry in its various forms thrived like never before. In a twist of fate, this time it was the British government that borrowed $2 billion from the Egyptians.

Iraq's Prime Minister suggested a union of the Arab countries in the "Fertile Crescent" and although this did not materialize, an Arab League was formed in 1944.

The First Palestine War

In May 1948 the Arab League went to war with Israel.

On May 14, 1948, the British Mandate officially expired. That same day, the Jewish National Council issued the Declaration of the Establishment of the State of Israel. About 10 minutes later, President Truman officially recognized the State of Israel, and the Soviet Union also quickly recognized Israel.

However, the Palestinians and the Arab League did not recognize the new state, and the very next day, armies from Egypt, Syria, Lebanon and Iraq invaded the former British Mandate to squelch Israel, while Saudi Arabia assisted the Arab armies. Jordan would also get involved in the war, fighting the Israelis around Jerusalem. Initially, the Arab armies numbered over 20,000 soldiers, but the Zionist militia groups like the Lehi, Irgun and Haganah made it possible for Israel to quickly assemble the Israel Defense Forces, still known today simply as the IDF. By the end of 1948, the Israelis had over 60,000 soldiers and the Arab armies numbered over 50,000.

The Israelis began pressing their advantages on both land and air by the fall of 1948, bombing foreign capitals like Damascus while overrunning Arab armies in the British Mandate. In towns like Ramat Rachel and Deir Yassin, close quarter combat in villages led to civilian casualties and charges of massacres. In particular, the Jewish assault on Deir Yassin, which led to the death of about 50 Palestinians, is often labeled a massacre by the Palestinians, although the Israelis asserted that house to house combat made fighting difficult.

Regardless, Palestinians who heard of the news of Jewish attacks on places like Deir Yassin were afraid for their lives and began to flee their homes. At the same time, Palestinians were encouraged by commanders of the Arab armies to clear out of the area until after they could defeat Israel. Palestinians and Jews had been fighting since 1947, and over 250,000 Palestinians had already fled their homes by the time the 1948 War had started. It is unclear how many Palestinians fled from Jewish forces and how many left voluntarily, but by the end of the war over 700,000 Palestinians had fled from their homes in the former British Mandate. Meanwhile, nearly 800,000 Jews had been forcibly expelled from their homes in nations throughout the Middle East, leading to an influx of Jews at the same time Palestinians were leaving.

In late 1948, Israel was on the offensive. That December, the U.N. General Assembly passed Resolution 194, which declared that under a peace agreement, "refugees wishing to return to their homes and live in peace with their neighbors should be permitted to do so," and "compensation should be paid for the property of those choosing not to return." Egypt was so unprepared they used the road maps obtained from an American car dealer, and one of Farouk's mistresses was suborned to pass information to Israel. The Egyptian army was ingloriously routed, 2,000 of its soldiers killed, and Egypt itself was only saved by the British refusing Israeli passage through the Canal Zone, the much-hated by Egypt provision which turned out to be their saviour.

Months later, Israel began signing armistices with Egypt, Jordan, and Syria, which left Israel in control of nearly 75% of the lands that were to be partitioned into the two states under the 1947 plan. Jordan now occupied Judea and Samaria, which later became known as the West Bank due to its position on the western bank of the Jordan River. Jordan also occupied three quarters of Jerusalem, with the Israelis controlling only about a quarter in the western part of the city. To the west, Egypt occupied the Gaza Strip.

The new armistice lines became known as the "Green Line."

Military Rule and Arab Nationalism (1952-1981)

Society of Muslim Brothers

In 1948 the Muslim Brotherhood had 2,000 branches in Egypt and provided education, medical clinics and general welfare for a large element of the poorer classes. The women's auxiliary, Muslim Sisters, and the youth branch, the Rovers (much like Boy Scouts), numbered 40,000. But there was a dark element, the Secret Apparatus, that committed assassinations and bombings. Their "Supreme Guide" was Sheikh Hasan al-Banna, who ordered the assassination of the Prime

Minister; in his turn he was murdered in 1949, presumed to have been killed by government agents. A crackdown ordered by Farouk left 4,000 members of the Brotherhood imprisoned in 1949, but in 1951 an appeal against the group's dissolution was upheld in the courts.

1950 Elections

In the 1950 elections, the Wafd came out ahead with 40% of the vote and set about a program of social reform. School fees were abolished, pensions for widows, orphans and the disabled were created, but plans to distribute land were not fulfilled.

In October 1951, Nahhas leading the Wafd abrogated the 1936 Anglo-Egyptian agreement, declared Farouk was king of both Egypt and the Sudan, and that the British had no further rights in the Canal Zone where Egyptian workers were obliged to go on strike. The Egyptian government immediately dismissed all British employees. In response to these measures, the British retaliated in January 1952 with an attack on the police headquarters in Ismailia, killing 50. Mob violence followed on "Black Saturday" with burning in Cairo of western type hotels and restaurants, including the famed Shepheard's Hotel. 30 people died, hundreds were injured, 400 buildings were destroyed, and the property damage cost $500 million. Eventually the Egyptian army took over, fires were extinguished, and Farouk dismissed the Wafd cabinet. Who was responsible remains unknown. It's probable that it was a spontaneous act that attracted unconnected groups.

Chaos followed, and there were four new governments in six months before Farouk's dismissal.

The Egyptian Officers Cabal

The defeat by Israel was a blow to Egyptian pride, but there were many changes in the Middle East at the time. There had been revolutions in Yemen in 1948, in Syria in 1949, King Abdullah of Jordan was assassinated in 1951, and many secret societies in Egypt plotted to do the same to King Farouk.

At one time a finishing school for the sons of the wealthy, the Egyptian Military Academy had altered its intake of students to those who succeeded in competitive examinations, which brought in a quite different societal group, many from financially modest origins. A "Free Officers Society" was formed, but its origins are disputed and may have initially been multiple groups. Regardless, it was organized along traditional conspiratory lines, in cells of five, and with a hierarchy spreading from each cell.

In 1951 their ethos was to: destroy the British occupation; eliminate feudalism; end the power of capitalism; create social equality; develop a strong people's army; and establish democracy. There was at that time no political party affiliation.

The Free Officers led a revolution in 1952, overthrowing the government on the night of July 22. The CIA, of course, was held responsible, but the actual revolution seems to have been a Keystone Cops affair. Answar Sadat didn't know the timing and had gone to the movies, and Gamal Abdel Nasser's car was stopped by the police because his tail light was not working. The opposition was even less ready, however, and King Farouk was instructed to abdicate. After the U.S. and British declined to help, Farouk willingly gave up power, his infant son was declared successor, and a regency council was installed.

Nasser

The Free Officers found not everyone thought as disinterestedly as they did. Nasser later wrote, "Every man we met sought nothing else but the destruction of another man." The Muslim Brotherhood demanded the Koran should be Egypt's constitution, while textile workers rioted and burnt their factories. In response, the military shot some and executed others.

Democracy was fine as a principle, but in short order the Free Officers concluded it was inefficient and seriously interfered with their views of progress. Parliament was dissolved in December 1952, and in June 1953 the last vestiges of monarchy were abolished. General Muhammad Naguib was elected President, Prime Minister, and Chairman of the Revolutionary Command Council (RCC). Members of the RCC assumed all senior government positions.

Gamal Abdel Nasser

With progressing internal rivalries, the aggressive Nasser came into conflict with Naguib, who resigned from the presidency in February 1954. This delighted Nasser, of course, but the people turned against Nasser and he was forced to ask Naguib to return to office. Nasser then so manipulated affairs that his own supporters took all significant offices, and although Naguib remained as President, he was stripped of any real power.

Possibly in relation to his imperfect demands for British evacuation of Suez, shots were fired at Nasser in Alexandria in 1954. The culprit was found to belong to the Muslim Brotherhood, he and a number of other supposed co-conspirators were executed, and a pogrom on the Brotherhood was initiated. President Naguib was arrested, and the office of President declared void.

Egypt had failed against Israel in the earlier war, and Israel continued to retaliate against incursions from Gaza, which was still Egyptian held. In one case, there was a bizarre, fortunately frustrated, affair in which Mossad agents planned to blow up American institutions in Cairo to damage US/Egyptian relations. Nasser wanted to equip his army to hold off Israel, but the British and Americans were not interested in helping him. In his turn he was not interested in joining the Baghdad Pact, effectively NATO for the Middle East, which he construed as in America's interests against Russia but did nothing for Egypt's concerns with Israel.

Thus, when Nasser attended a conference of "non-aligned" nations, he was ripe for the communist picking, and in September 1955 an agreement was made with Czechoslovakia (a Soviet satellite) for a $200 million worth of arms, to be bought with cotton.

Aswan High Dam

Dating back to the first years of the 20th century, Britain had helped to improve the Nile Valley irrigation, extensively increasing the available arable land. One such project, opened in 1902, was the Aswan Dam, which had been elevated in height twice since its first formation. Plans to put dams on the White Nile would have left Egypt at the mercy of Sudan, and they were discounted even though they were sound from an engineering viewpoint. The ultimate decision was to make a new and even higher dam at Aswan, from which year round irrigation of an additional million acres, and huge electrical resources, were anticipated. The drawback was the billion dollars it would cost.

The World Bank offered to fund the first phase, partly supported by the U.S. and the U.K., but both countries attached strings – control over Egypt's economy, no arms deals, and no contracts with communist countries. In June 1956 the Soviets offered Nasser $1,120,000,000 at 2% interest for the construction of the dam. Egypt hesitantly agreed to the conditions imposed effectively by the U.S., but the day after their consent was obtained, John Foster Dulles, U.S. Secretary of State, cancelled the American offer. Nasser felt they'd made a fool of him.

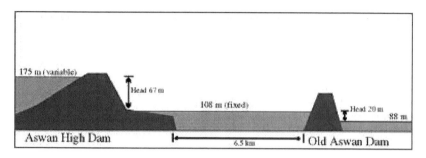

In direct response, in July 1956 Nasser invaded and occupied the Suez Canal Zone, announced the Canal was to be nationalized, and the tolls charged would be used to pay for the Aswan High Dam. Not generally recognized by the world, the Canal did in fact belong to Egypt. Although there were shareholders for the seized property, appropriate compensation was offered. The British were convinced the Egyptians were incapable of running the affairs of the Canal, but the Egyptians proved them wrong.

Britain and France, together with Israel, set up an invasion force, but the lack of support from President Eisenhower and the opposition of the Commonwealth nations deterred them and the invasion was called off. Egypt was left in charge of her own Canal, and Nasser was the hero of the day. There followed an ugly period of expulsion of French, British and Israeli citizens and companies from Egypt.

Meanwhile the government of Egypt underwent radical changes. With a new constitution women were given the vote, political parties were banned, and there was to be one voice only, the National Union.

In 1958 the Soviet Union provided funding for the Aswan High Dam project.

Arab Nationalism

After the Suez Canal War, Egyptian leader Gamal Abdel Nasser envisioned creating a unified Arab world, commonly referred to as pan-Arabism. Nasser was the consummate pan-Arab leader in the 1960s, positioning himself as the leader of the Arab world through increasing incitement against Israel with rhetoric. Most Egyptians thought of themselves as Egyptians and only Egyptians, but Nasser concluded there was a potential for group strength by his declaration that Egypt was a member of the Arab nations. From this sprang a short lived union with Syria, to form the United Arab Republic (UAR), in which Syria very much played second fiddle and eventually withdrew in September 1961.

For a time a spirit of "pan-Arabism" was popular, but this movement, nebulous in itself, was redefined as Arab socialism and widely interpreted as state ownership of land and property, not unlike Mehmet Ali's control of Egypt. Pan-Arabism would also take another blow during the Six Day War.

June 1967 war

Israel found itself in possession of more land after 1948 than envisioned by the U.N. Partition Plan, but the Green Line still left it less than 10 miles wide in some positions. In the summer of 1967, the armies of Jordan and Syria mobilized near Israel's borders, while Egypt's army mobilized in the Sinai Peninsula just west of the Gaza Strip. Combined, the Arab armies numbered over 200,000 soldiers.

In early June 1967, the Israelis captured Jordanian intelligence that indicated an invasion was imminent. When Nasser declared an embargo to shipping through the Tiran Straits at the opening to the Gulf of Aqaba. Israel responded on June 5 by a pre-emptive air strike against the Egyptian planes on the ground and destroyed 80% of the Egyptian Air Force. In three days the Israeli army took the Sinai peninsula and 5000 Egyptian soldiers were prisoner, 20,000 died mostly from neglect by their officers, some of battle wounds. On June 8, the Israeli army halted at the east bank of the Gulf of Suez. The Suez Canal was closed.

Over the course of a war lasting less than a week, the Israelis had overwhelmed the Egyptians in the west, destroying thousands of tanks and capturing the Gaza Strip and the entire Sinai Peninsula. At the same time, Israel drove the Jordanians out of Jerusalem and the West Bank, and it captured the Golan Heights from Syria near the border of Lebanon. Israel had tripled the size of the lands it controlled and had gone from less than 10 miles wide in some spots to over 200 miles wide from the Sinai Peninsula to the West Bank. Israel also unified Jerusalem.

As with the 1948 war, the 1967 war ended with an armistice, creating war heroes out of Yitzhak Rabin and Ariel Sharon. Nasser in shame resigned his posts, but the people of Egypt begged him to reconsider, and he returned to office.

The hand of the USSR was also strengthened as the Arab states now found themselves more reliant on the Soviets for arms. The policy of "3 No's" developed – *no negotiation; no recognition; no peace with Israel*. There followed prolonged skirmishing at sea and in the air over the Suez Canal and adjacent Egyptian air space, called the "War of Attrition."

Nasser died unexpectedly in September 1970, bringing Sadat to power.

Anwar Sadat

Anwar Sadat was Vice-President and the logical successor to Nasser, but he was not highly regarded despite being voted into that position. Unexpectedly he proved himself more forthright than expected and fired Nasser's former associates, gaining popularity when he discharged Nasser's secret agents and made a bonfire of the secret information they had amassed.

Initially, Sadat continued Nasser's policy of friendship with the USSR, and Egypt continued to receive military supplies from them. Eventually, however, Sadat came to resent the domineering attitude of the Soviets and their continuing control of some of the armaments supplied to him.

October (Yom Kippur) War

On October 6, 1973, Syria and Egypt caught Israel off guard during the Jewish holy holiday of Yom Kippur, surprise attacking the Sinai Peninsula and Golan Heights. Although they initially made gains, the Israelis turned the tide within a week, going on the counteroffensive and winning the war within 3 weeks. The Israelis crossed the Suez Canal and were within an hour's drive of Cairo when a cease-fire was agreed, leaving Israel soldiers on the Egyptian side of the canal, and Egyptian soldiers, surrounded by Israelis, in the Sinai.

The Yom Kippur War was the last concerted invasion of Israel by conventional Arab armies, but it underscored how entangled the West and the Soviet Union had gotten in the region. The British and French had been allied with Israel in the 1950s, including during the Suez Canal War, and the United States assisted Israel by providing weapons as early as the 1960s. As a way of counteracting Western influence, the Soviets developed ties with the Arab nations.

For Egypt, the military benefit was a minus, but the psychological benefit inadvertently proved enormous. After years tolerating an Israeli occupation of the Sinai, and effective blockage of the Suez Canal, the Arab oil producing countries said they would progressively reduce output by 5%

a month, and an embargo on the U.S. until Israel withdrew. Iran followed suit by raising prices. Eventually, after much shuttle diplomacy by U.S. Secretary of State Henry Kissinger, an agreement was reached by which the Israelis withdrew to 10 miles east of the Canal.

The limited success achieved in forcing Israeli withdrawal, attributed by the Egyptians to Sadat, caused a boom in building along the Canal, opportunities for investment in Egypt, a swing away from socialist government control in the direction of free enterprise, and tentative easing of relations with the US. For a number of reasons, including some just listed, the USSR reduced and then cancelled military aid.

However, increasing wealth and job opportunities in other Arab states resulted in a significant outflowing of Egyptian labor and professional talent, bringing on debt that once again led to more than half the state's incomes going to repayments. At the suggestion of the IMF, subsidies to food and fuel were reduced with significant rise in prices, particularly in regard to bread since Egypt was importing half of what it consumed.

The Camp David Accords - Peace with Israel

Sadat undertook an almost unbelievable mission. Addressing the People's Assembly in November 1977, he made what was probably a rhetorical claim: he was prepared to go to the Knesset in Jerusalem to seek peace. Walter Cronkite asked if he meant it, and Sadat said he did. Cronkite asked Prime Minister Begin of Israel if he would accept such a visit, and he said he would.

Sadat flew to Israel, was received with every courtesy, addressed the Knesset and flew back to Egypt to a great welcome. To everyone's surprise Begin came to Egypt on Christmas Day when he met with President Carter and Sadat. After the Yom Kippur War, President Carter's administration sought to establish a peace process that would settle the conflict in the Middle East, while also reducing Soviet influence in the region. On September 17, 1978, after secret negotiations at the presidential retreat Camp David, Egyptian President Anwar Sadat and Israeli Prime Minister Menachem Begin signed a peace treaty between the two nations, in which Israel ceded the Sinai Peninsula to Egypt in exchange for a normalization of relations, making Egypt the first Arab adversary to officially recognize Israel. Carter also tried to create a peace process that would settle the rest of the conflict vis-à-vis the Israelis and Palestinians, but it never got off the ground.

For the Camp David Accords, Begin and Sadat won the Nobel Peace Prize, but the peace treaty, did not raise Egypt's popularity with other Arab states, noticeably not with the Palestinians.

Begin, Carter and Sadat at the signing ceremony

Naturally, the peace treaty and the negotiations that led up to it brought Egypt closer to the US side of the Cold War, and the U.S. began supplying arms and aid to Egypt. This aid was not in large enough quantities to endanger Israel, but enough that the Egyptian military could enjoy the pleasure of playing with their military hardware. Tourism, a vital industry for Egypt, was also revived.

However, the negative aspect to life came from increasing numbers of young persons with education but no work available to their level of learning. And inevitably this breeds discontent. There developed increasing numbers of secret societies with fundamental Islamism as their tenets, in parallel with changes occurring in Iran. Leaders were captured and often imprisoned if not executed, and Islamic forms of dress, previously uncommon, were adopted. Beards were grown, attempts were made in the universities to separate the sexes, and plots were hatched to kill Sadat. Increasingly, suppression became the order of the day.

Since 1977, party politics had been restored, the Wafd party returned, and the Muslim Brotherhood was permitted to have representatives as individuals but not as a party since religion was banned as a political party issue. Still, only the National Democratic Party was of consequence.

The peace treaty with Israel eventually cost Sadat his life. At a military parade, October 6, 1981, Sadat was in the stands taking the salute. A young officer jumped out of a truck, surprising those in the stands totally unaware of his intentions, and he began shooting at Sadat with an AK-47. The military officers responsible for the assassination had ties to the opposition group Muslim Brotherhood, as well as Ayman al-Zawahiri, who later became one of the senior leaders of al-Qaeda and the new head upon Osama bin Laden's death.

The Hosni Mubarak Years

The day after Sadat's murder, the Assembly appointed the Vice President, General Hosni Mubarak to succeed to the President's post, as the fourth in that role in Egypt. He had previously served in the Air Force, was highly regarded as an administrator, had been Vice President since 1975, and had been sent on a number of diplomatic missions to Heads of State representing Sadat. Mubarak was among those wounded when Sadat was killed.

Mubarak entered into his tasks in a quiet way, first improving social conditions with an increase in low cost housing and state subsidised production of clothing, furniture, and medicine. He walked a fine line, trying to keep the friendship and financial support of both the USSR and the U.S., as well as the difficulty of placating Israel without offending the Palestinians and the Arab powers.

Many of the strictures imposed by Sadat were removed and political prisoners were released. He did, however, crack down on Islamists, particularly the Muslim Brotherhood, and many were jailed. The previously tolerated outward signs were banned, including beards, galabias (male gowns) and female head scarves on university campuses.

1984 USSR and USA

Relationships with the USSR were improved, and the terms for repayment of debt were eased; ambassadors were exchanged after 1984. The US continued to support Egypt financially, between one and three billion dollars a year, represented by arms, capital goods and food, and some capital improvements in substructures as well as social assistance.

1985 Achille Lauro

On October 7, 1985, four Palestinian terrorists hijacked the Achille Lauro liner off Egypt and threw a handicapped Leon Klinghoffer (an American Jew) overboard. They were refused permission to dock in Syria, but after negotiations they were permitted to dock in Port Said, and after two days of negotiations, the Egyptian government compromised with an offer of immunity to the Palestinians who were to be flown to Tunisia aboard an Egyptian commercial airliner. President Reagan, however, ordered U.S. fighter planes to force the Egyptian civilian plane to land at a NATO base in Italy.

On October 10th there was a stand-off between the Italian Carabinieri and U.S. Special Forces, including SEAL Team 6. The Carabinieri prevailed, but diplomatic relations between Italy and the US were severely strained, as they were with Egypt, for which the U.S. had rather less concern.

1989 Arab League membership restored

The other Arab states gradually came to accept Egypt's working relations with Israel, and without much said, their own relations with Egypt were restored. Egypt was the only state to have had its membership suspended in the Arab League, but in 1989 Egypt was restored to its prior position and the offices of the League returned to Cairo.

1991 Gulf War

Mubarak lent his services to ameliorate the tense relations between Saddam Hussein's Iraq and

Kuwait in an effort to prevent the invasion, then to try to stop the invasion. Finally he provided 40,000 Egyptian soldiers to drive Saddam out of Kuwait during Operation Desert Storm. The Egyptian infantry were among the first in Saudi Arabia, and their lead encouraged support from other Arab nations.

2003 Iraq War

President Mubarak argued against the invasion of Iraq, believing the issue the Arabs had with Israel was of greater priority. Mubarak also asserted that destroying one bin Laden would only produce a hundred more. Once the die was cast, though, he did not advocate an immediate pull-out of U.S. forces, knowing chaos would ensue. Furthermore, there was nothing to be gained by criticizing the Americans too harshly when receiving so much aid from them.

2005 Election

Mubarak was re-elected by majority votes of Assembly in 1987, 1993, and 1999. In the 2005 election it was determined the President would be chosen by popular vote, as in the U.S. Naturally, there were substantiated complaints of vote rigging and corruption, and when one of the rival candidates, dissident Ayman Nour, had the temerity to complain, he was convicted of forgery and sentenced to five years.

Assassination attempts

At least six attempts were made to kill Mubarak after he was made President, mostly involving various extremist Islamic groups. In turn, those groups were severely suppressed, to the extent that as many as 20,000 persons were probably incarcerated, and there was no question that police standards failed to meet the requirements of a civilized society. However, it was found in 2005 that 72 of the elected deputies, who stood as individuals, were in fact Muslim Brotherhood members, a sign of the reach of Egypt's largest and most organized opposition group.

An Emergency Law dating to 1967 gave the police, who were directed by the army and the ruling clique of generals, virtually unrestrained powers. In effect, there were no civil rights and anyone could be (and often were) imprisoned without explanation. Numbers are indefinite but there may have been 30,000 persons held in this manner in Mubarak's police state.

The military undoubtedly believed it when they said such measures were necessary to control Islamic extremism, including the Muslim Brotherhood.

State corruption during Mubarak's presidency:

Police states always seem to foster corruption, resulting in rules that are impossible to observe and payments made to petty officials to evade punishment for them.

On a larger scale, absolute power corrupts absolutely. At his trial it was alleged Mubarak had money tucked away in the amount of many billions of dollars.

Muslim Brotherhood

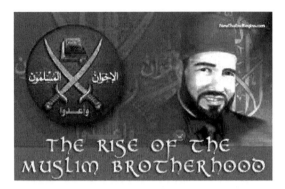

The Muslim Brotherhood was a thorn in the side of Egypt's secular rulers for generations, and now they stand on the precipice of power in Egypt with Mubarak's removal. Naturally, that means more attention than ever is being paid to them.

The Muslim Brotherhood bases its beliefs on its own interpretation of the Koran, and not unlike fundamental Christians who can find whatever they please in the Bible, fundamental Islamists can find whatever they please in the Koran.

The Brotherhood was started as a movement in 1928 by Hassan al-Banna with the excellently expressed intentions of coupling the teaching of Islam with the practice of good deeds – not unlike mendicant friars and the better monasteries of the Christian Middle Ages. But good intentions were not enough, and political involvement followed. If you believed the problems of the poor were because the British wanted them that way, what was more logical than to oppose the British? And if the British were driven out, why not all infidels? The drive became to establish that "Islam is the solution," and the law would be the Sharia.

The Brotherhood flourished in the early and mid-20th century by providing much needed social services, schools, sports and medical facilities, and in 20 years it had grown to a membership of 2 million. But al-Banna, who was assassinated in 1948, saw fit to form a paramilitary force, called "Special Apparatus," and he used them in "terrorist" actions against the British and the Jews, but also against leading Egyptians such as the Prime Minister.

In 1948, while the British were still in Egypt, the Muslem Brotherhood was banned. In 1952, when the Free Officers had their own revolution, the Muslim Brotherhood came into favor again, since they had all worked in the "underground" together. There followed an on-again off-again relationship with government. The Brotherhood (aka the Ikhwan) were popular and numerically powerful; they had a component that wished to serve the needy, but they also had "activists" who thought killing the opposition was the way to go, and promoted *jihad* (struggle) as the preferable way of life.

Thus, periodically the Brotherhood was part of the mainstream political system, as in 1984 when they allied with the Wafd party, 1987 when they allied with Labor and Liberal parties, and in 2000 they held 17 seats in the Assembly. But Mubarak was concerned with the rise in legitimate representation of the party he feared, and a law was passed proscribing any party with religious affiliation. With that, many members of the Brotherhood were arrested, effectively for no better reason than their membership in the party.

The Arab Spring

Tunisia seemed like a weird place for the removal of Mubarak to have its origins. In Sidi Bouzid, a small central Tunisian town of no consequence, there was a 26 years old barrow boy who was no more important than his town, but whose name will now linger in the history books. Mohamed Bouazizi's father was dead and Mohamed was the sole support of his family of eight. He had for seven years made their living by selling vegetables from a handcart and stall.

Although he should have been licensed, licences were not obtainable and periodically he paid off the corrupt police to the cost of five dollars, a day's wages. From what he earned he kept his family fed and his sisters in school. But on December 17, 2010, a female police officer not only confiscated his cart and produce but also insulted the memory of his deceased father. Although one might have expected Mohamed to know better, he went to the office of the local authorities to complain about his treatment and the inability to get properly licensed, which led to recurring harassment. The female office worker refused him permission to talk to anyone in authority and slapped him for daring to complain. One can only speculate on how he felt or why he did it, but Mohamed doused himself in gasoline, and set fire to himself outside the gates of the building in which he had been so insulted.

Mohamed was taken first to the local hospital which was not equipped to deal with injuries such as his, so he was driven 70 miles to the city of Sfax where he was treated. Because his self-immolation was gaining notoriety, he was transferred to a hospital near Tunis where he was visited by President Ben Ali. Mohamed lived in agony for two weeks, then died on January 4, 2011. During the two weeks he lingered, there was increasing unrest in Tunisia. Disturbances were not unknown, but they were not everyday events, and they were usually suppressed without bloodshed. Freedom to express an opinion was, however, very definitely not part of Tunisian life. Lahseen Naji had suffered death by accidental electrocution on December 22nd when he climbed a power tower during a demonstration, and on the 24th Mohamed Ammari was shot dead by police in one of several demonstrations across Tunisia. On 14th January, 2011, President Zine al-Abidine Ben Ali of Tunisia and his family left the country, reportedly taking a plane load of gold with them.

Though he certainly could not have intended it, Mohammed Bouazizi quite unconsciously set off what became designated as the "Arab Spring." It came about gradually but mounted and mounted until it could not be denied. Mohamed Bouazizi died in Tunis on January 4th 2011, but in the three weeks that passed between the times of his self-injury and his death, the world had been apprised of the issues and the internet was abuzz with gossip. Hand held communications characterized these revolutions like never before – Twitter and Facebook were sovereign – although they had been known to be used in coordinating mob activities in the "protests" in western cities such as London and Toronto.

It was expected that the protests in Tunisia would spread to other countries, and Mohamed ElBaradei, known to the West for his activities in nuclear weapons inspections, had prophetically forecasted they would appear in his own country, Egypt. And they did – much of it played out before the well placed television cameras with continuous "real time" coverage of the action in Tahrir Square and the long bridge over the River Nile.

The movement in Egypt took hold on January 25th 2011 with what was known to them as The Day of Revolt. Although it was Cairo that was seen on the western TV, there were protests against President Hosni Mubarak all over the country. To some extent they faced off with the police, on the whole they were non-violent. But in the next two days it began to get ugly, stones were thrown, shots were fired, a few hundred were injured and a very small number killed; barbed wire went up and corrugated iron sheets were used by the most aggressive of the protestors.

Tahrir Square in Cairo is a large open area, adjacent to one of the several bridges over the Nile. It must have been supposed by the authorities that they would disperse and go about their business, but day by day the crowds grew, they did not disperse, and they called for the government to fall. Some said they would remain in the Square until President Mubarak resigned.

Friday after the believers leave the mosques is the traditional time for mob action in the Muslim world. On 28th January, which they termed Friday of Rage, the authorities had pre-emptively closed down communication devices, but the protestors in thousands gathered in public spaces such as Tahrir Square. The army, in general more sympathetic with the people, was called in to reinforce the police numbers. It was a very big, but a relatively non-hostile gathering which continued in the demand Mubarak should go. Progressively as numbers increased, so did the feelings of hostility, and there were threatening displays of military might.

Tahrir Square in February 2011

President Mubarak discharged his entire cabinet, and although on TV he sympathised with the demands of the protestors, he also defended the attempt to suppress the protest. President Obama called President Mubarak, and advised him to "give meaning" to promises to improve the lot of the people of Egypt.

On 29th January, President Mubarak appointed his intelligence chief, Omar Suleiman, as Vice President, and the Air Minister, Ahmed Shafiq, as Prime Minister, confirming there was no intention of the military to relinquish control of government. They would only change the seating. The crowds became less satisfied, overt fighting occurred with the police and to a lesser extent the army, and there was now reported a total of 74 deaths.

The last day of January was given a slogan type name even before the event: The March of the Millions. How many came to Tahrir Square was impossible to tell since capacity was a quarter of that, but the TV certainly showed it packed. Mubarak promised to cut short his Presidency, but the crowd was not satisfied and predictably the mood became ugly on both sides. That same day, the army (which had always been considered a "people's army") declared the people had legitimate rights and they would not use force against them.

As unrest mounted, February 2nd became the Battle of the Camel, and television viewers were treated to a bizarre scene of men mounted on horses and camels riding aggressively into the mob, inciting further violence. The crowds got more assertive, less holiday-like, and destructive forces came into play. The headquarters of the governing NDP party was torched and other government offices were invaded. 26 deaths were reported.

As February unrolled, the crowds increased, noticeably in Tahrir Square, but also elsewhere in Egypt; "march of a million" became a popular slogan. The competence of many Egyptians to express themselves lucidly in English facilitated TV interviews. And President Mubarak announced his term of office would constitutionally cease in September 2011 and would not seek re-election. Obviously Mubarak did not understand the "mood of the mob," which wanted him out of office in minutes, not months. Following on the President's directions, the Army told the people their message had been heard and they should now go home, but they didn't. And it began, inevitably, to grow more violent, with the throwing of Molotov cocktails and armoured personnel carriers very visible as a threat on the Square.

There followed a week of uncertainty, government resignations that didn't happen, and unheeded demands for Mubarak to go. Then, on 11th February, nearly three weeks after the protests began, Vice-President Omar Suleiman announced the resignation of President Mubarak, with immediate effect. Joy in Tahrir Square was unbridled. Mubarak let it be known he would not leave Egypt, and it was found he and his family had gone to Sharm el-Sheikh on the Red Sea. Power, however, continued to rest with the generals, and on further analysis it was unclear what had been achieved.

Further career of Hosni Mubarak

At the end of February, the courts issued an unnecessary order prohibiting Mubarak from leaving Egypt and placing him under house arrest in a palace. In April the courts announced he was to be questioned for charges of corruption and abuse of power, and in May the charges were escalated to premeditated murder of the Tahrir Square protestors. By this time it was evident Mubarak's health was fading, always with the *caveat* that health issues are commonly used to escape legal retribution.

At the end of May he was found, *in absentia*, guilty of the nebulous charge of shutting down communication via the internet and fined $35 million.

In August, Mubarak was brought to court on a stretcher and held in a cage while the trial proceeded with charges of murder, for which Egypt still exacts the death penalty. He was ordered held in a military hospital while court proceedings unfolded, which they did very gradually, perhaps too slowly.

What had started as a show trial concluded without TV coverage and reached rather peculiar conclusions. Mubarak was found not guilty of ordering the actions to control the protest, but guilty of failing to stop it when it had started. The penalty was to be life imprisonment.

Mubarak and his family were absolved of all charges relating to finance, despite rumors they had skimmed up to $70 billion from public funds.

All police who were charged with Mubarak in relation to deaths of protestors were found not guilty by virtue of insufficient evidence. Unsurprisingly the crowds were not satisfied.

Omar Suleiman

Suleiman was appointed Vice President by President Hosni Mubarak on 29 January 2011. Undoubtedly Mubarak had good reasons in his own mind for this choice, but since Suleiman was Head of Intelligence, and Intelligence had an extremely unsavory reputation for torture (some in association with the CIA rendition program), he was obviously not going to be the people's choice.

On 11 February 2011, it was given to Suleiman to announce Mubarak's resignation. However, he did not move into the position of President, as that power was transferred to the Armed Forces Supreme Council.

Suleiman withdrew altogether from politics and on 19 July 2012 died in a United States hospital.

2012 Election

There were two candidates of note, and with the expectation of biased polling it was expected Ahmed Shafiq, the former chief of the air force and prime minister under President Hosni Mubarak, would be the clear victor.

The Muslim Brotherhood openly ran their candidate, Khairat al-Shater, a millionaire businessman and deputy leader of the Brotherhood. It was thought he might be disqualified and prevented from running, which in fact was the case. Mohammed Mursi was originally the reserve candidate for the Muslim Brotherhood, and he did not put in his nomination papers until the very last day. After al-Shater was declared ineligible, the Brotherhood undertook to support Mohammed Mursi.

Unsurprisingly, he was one of the two candidates at the peak of counting, taking 24% of vote in the first round in May, and thus he was one of the two in the constitutionally provided run off. In the run-off, the vote was declared to have been 51.73% in Mursi's favor, and he was to be the 5th President of Egypt. Thus, on June 30, 2012, Mohammed Mursi was sworn in as the first ever democratically elected President of Egypt.

Mursi is a 60-year-old engineer who studied at Cairo University in the 1970s, then in the United States took further studies for his PhD at the University of Southern California. He was also an Assistant Professor at California State University from 1982 to 1985. Two of his children were born in the U.S. and are therefore citizens there. When he returned to Egypt he was made head of the engineering department at Zagazig University.

Mursi, like many professionals, associated himself with the Muslim Brotherhood. When they were not allowed membership as a party, he served as an independent in the Assembly from 2000 to 2005, when he lost his seat in what may have been an unfair electoral process.

The Brotherhood chose him as their spokesperson, and after Hosni Mubarak resigned he was appointed chairman of the Freedom and Justice Party, which won the majority of seats in both the upper and lower houses of Assembly.

There is always fear of extremist Islamism associated with the Brotherhood, and Mursi has said he will institute the Brotherhood's slogan, "Islam is the solution." At the same time, he has claimed he has plans for moderation. Whether the two are compatible remains to be seen, but he has rejected any idea he would turn Egypt into a theocracy. He has said he looks for a new constitution to protect civil rights, but at the same time follow the tenets of Islamic law.

Hisham Qandil

Egypt's President Mohammed Mursi has asked Hisham Qandil, the minister of water resources in the current government, to become the country's youngest prime minister since Gamal Abdul Nasser in 1954. He is not from the Muslim Brotherhood, but as a rival politician has explained, Mursi "brought in someone who is not from the Brotherhood, but whose ideology is similar."

It is not clear how much power Mr Qandil will have. A decree issued in June gave the Supreme Council of the Armed Forces all legislative power and veto power on matters relating to national security, while the president will have final say on key appointments and policies. In point of fact, despite the dramatic changes since Tahrir Square, the generals are still running Egypt.

Qandil has a background similar to Mursi. He is a graduate in engineering from Cairo University, has a PhD from North Carolina, and has been a bureaucrat at the ministry of water resources and irrigation's National Water Research Centre (NWRC), a matter of vital interest in Egypt. He has said his will be a government of technocrats who will have professional competence and will not tolerate corruption.

However, the choice of members for his cabinet does not altogether bear out his words, and the generals remain. Of the 18 ministers named, two are members of the Muslim Brotherhood's Freedom and Justice Party (FJP). Major-Gen Ahmed Jamal al-Din will be interior minister, Foreign Minister Mohammed Kamal Amr and Finance Minister Mumtaz al-Said will keep their posts; Field Marshal Mohammed Hussein Tantawi, the head of the ruling Supreme Council of the Armed Forces (Scaf), will be defence minister; Mustafa Musaad will be education minister; Tariq Wafiq, head of the FJP's housing committee, will be housing minister; the minister of religious endowments will be Osama al-Abd, the president of al-Azhar University.

Egypt has changed, but how much remains to be seen. The new President is a member of an Islamist party that has been known for both its social values and its tendency to assassinate. The new Prime Minister has been chosen in the President's image. And yet real power still remains with the generals, and it is highly questionable whether any fundamental changes have occurred.

Made in the USA
Lexington, KY
30 October 2016